Berger Science Readers

GROWL!

A Book About
BEARS

For Cathy and Marv, with a great big "bear" hug
—M.B.

Special thanks to Laurie Roulston
of the Denver Museum of Natural History
for her expertise

Photography credits:

Cover: Johnny Johnson/Tony Stone Images; pages 3-4: Erwin & Peggy Bauer;
page 5: Bill Lea/DPA; page 7: Johnny Johnson/Tony Stone Images; page 8:
Claudia Adams/DPA; page 9: Stephen J. Krasemann/Photo Researchers;
page 10: Tom McHugh/Photo Researchers; page 11: Zig Leszczynski/Animals
Animals; page 12: Gijsbert van Frankenhuyzen/DPA; page 13: Erwin & Peggy
Bauer; page 14: Russ Gutshall/DPA; page 15: Rod Planck/DPA; pages 16-17:
Erwin & Peggy Bauer; page 19: Kevin Schafer/Tony Stone Images; page 20:
Jeanne Drake/Tony Stone Images; page 21: Yva Momatiuk & John Eastcott/
Photo Researchers; pages 22-24: Lynn & Donna Rogers; page 25: Michael
Giannechini/Photo Researchers; page 27: Russ Gutshall/DPA; page 28: Doug
Locke/DPA; page 29: Leonard Lee Rue III/Tony Stone Images; pages 30-32:
Lynn & Donna Rogers; page 33: Erwin & Peggy Bauer; page 34: Bruce M.
Herman/Photo Researchers; page 35: Bill Lea/DPA; page 37: Erwin & Peggy
Bauer; page 38: Fritz Polking/DPA; page 39: Erwin & Peggy Bauer

ISBN 0-439-80183-4

17 16 15 14 13   13 14/0

Printed in the U.S.A.   40
First revised edition, September 2005

Berger Science Readers

GROWL!

A Book About
BEARS

by Melvin & Gilda Berger

SCHOLASTIC INC.
New York Toronto London Auckland Sydney
Mexico City New Delhi Hong Kong Buenos Aires

Chapter One

What Do Bears Eat?

In *Goldilocks and the Three Bears*, the bears eat porridge. But real bears eat much more than that. And they're hungry all the time!

There are about eight different kinds of bears. Each kind has its own favorite foods.

The **grizzly bear** is one kind of bear. Grizzly bears feed on:

- nuts and berries,

- roots and plants,

- fish,

- small animals,

- and even bigger animals like young deer.

All this food adds up. Each grizzly eats as much as 35 pounds of food every day. It takes you almost three weeks to eat that much!

Grizzly bears eat a lot because they're so big. A grizzly can grow to be as long as a motorcycle. It can weigh as much as four grown–ups!

Polar bears eat mostly seals. Sometimes they hunt walruses. They also feed on fish and whales that have died.

Polar bears live where it's very cold. Eating lots of food helps them keep warm. So does a thick layer of fat under their skin.

Most bears like to eat honey. But **sun bears** really love the sweet stuff. That's why they're sometimes called honey bears. Sun bears also eat lots of birds, berries, and insects.

Sun bears are the smallest bears. Most are a little longer than a yardstick. They weigh about as much as a fifth grader. Sun bears spend much of their time climbing and resting in trees.

Sloth bears hunt ants and termites. The bears break open the nests. Then they stick out their long tongue. SLURP! They suck up the bugs. What loud noises the sloth bears make!

Sloth bears move very slowly. That's how they got their name. "Sloth" is an old English word that means "slow."

Giant pandas eat mostly bamboo. Without bamboo, they would starve.

Giant pandas have chubby white bodies with black marks. They have six fingers on their front paws. The extra finger is like a thumb. It helps them hold the bamboo.

People once thought giant pandas were big raccoons. Now most say that pandas are really bears.

Chapter Two

How Do Bears Find Food?

All bears have a big nose called a snout. Can you guess how this helps them fill their tummies with food?

A large snout gives bears a sharp
sense of smell. It helps them find food.
Did you know that some bears can sniff
a person from a mile away? They can
smell a dead animal at 12 miles!

Bears travel far to find something to eat. But they don't walk on their toes like most other animals. Instead, bears walk with their feet flat on the ground. They walk the same way you do—except on four feet.

Bears can also stand on two legs. This makes them much taller. It helps them get food that is hard to reach. And it helps them fight off enemies.

Most bears look fat and clumsy. Don't let their size fool you. Bears are very fast runners. A big bear can charge its prey at 40 miles an hour! That's faster than a horse can gallop. Few animals can escape a charging bear.

Except for the panda, bears have five toes on each paw. And every toe ends in a long, sharp claw. The claws always stick out. Bears use their claws to:

- dig for roots,
- climb trees,
- pick fruits and berries,
- and catch other animals.

Bears are powerful animals. One blow from a front paw can kill a deer. They can carry the dead animal a long, long way.

Bears also have huge, hairy heads. Their mouths are full of big teeth. The pointed front teeth rip into animals they eat. The flat back teeth grind up roots and plants.

Bears are very big. Their long,
shaggy hair makes them look even
bigger. Yet, bears are mostly gentle.
Except—when a person or animal
comes near their young or their food.
Then, watch out! Bears can get very
angry very fast.

Chapter Three

How Do Most Bears Get Ready for Winter?

In the fall, most bears eat more than usual. Every day they stuff themselves with food. They eat so much that they get very fat.

The bears then look for places to spend the winter. A bear's winter home is called a den. A den may be:

- a cave,
- a hollow tree,
- a space under a big rock,
- a shelter of twigs,
- or a hole dug in the snow.

Soon the weather turns very cold.
The bears can't find enough to eat.
One day it starts to snow. The bears
head for their dens. They curl up and
fall fast asleep!

All winter long, the bears don't eat or drink. They live off the fat in their body. They snore the days and nights away!

The bears sleep for a long time. But they wake easily. A loud noise may startle them awake.

Bears sometimes wake up on warm winter days. They crawl out of their dens. They may walk around for a while. Then the bears head back to their dens. Before you can say "good night," they're snoring again.

Bears *really* wake up when it's spring Then they shuffle out of their dens. At first, they're very thirsty. They drink lots of water. Sometimes there is still snow on the ground. The bears eat snow that melts in their mouths.

Then the bears look for food. They sniff the ground in search of plants and roots. They find fruits and nuts on bushes and trees. They catch and eat lots of fish, insects, and small animals.

Some other animals also sleep all winter. We say they hibernate (HI·ber·nate). Bats, frogs, and snakes hibernate. They stay asleep for the whole winter. They breathe very slowly. Their hearts beat much slower. Their temperatures drop way down.

But do bears really hibernate?
Bears sleep lightly and wake easily.
Their breathing and heartbeat
slow down only a little. And their
temperature stays nearly the same.

Some people say bears hibernate.
Some people say bears just take a long
nap. What do you think?

Chapter Four

When Are Baby Bears Born?

Most bear babies are born in the middle of winter. The mother gives birth in the den during her winter sleep. She usually has two babies at a time. They are called cubs.

The cubs are tiny. Each one looks like a rat without a tail. It usually weighs less than a pound. Human babies weigh far more at birth.

Bear cubs are helpless when they are born. Their eyes are closed. They have no teeth. They have no fur. And they can't walk.

The cubs stay in the den for about
two months. The mother bear snuggles
them close to her. She keeps her babies
toasty warm. And she feeds them milk
from her body.

The cubs grow bigger and bigger.
In spring, the bears come out of
their dens. The cubs are bouncy
and full of fun. Bear cubs and their
mother play together.

The mother teaches her cubs to hunt for food. She fights off any animal that comes too close.

A mother black bear teaches her cubs to climb trees. The cubs feed on nuts and fruits. They stay there until she calls them down.

A mother polar bear teaches her cubs to swim. She also shows them how to catch fish. Often she gives the cubs rides on her back.

A mother sun bear shows her cubs how to hunt at night. She also helps them make a bed of branches in a tree. They sleep there during the day.

All bear cubs stay close to their mothers for a long while. Some stay for several months. Some stay for a few years.

In time, the cubs can care for themselves. They find their own food. They look for mates.

Life for the bears goes on and on. All spring, summer, and fall, the hungry bears eat and eat. When winter comes, they crawl into dens. They go to sleep. Of course, they snore.

The mother bears have cubs. They feed and cuddle their babies. If bears dream, they dream of spring.
Sweet dreams, big and little bears!

Index